LOOKING AT ANTS

Dorothy Hinshaw Patent

Holiday House / New York

Library of Congress Cataloging-in-Publication Data

Patent, Dorothy Hinshaw.
Looking at ants/written by Dorothy Hinshaw Patent.— 1st ed.
p.   cm.
Summary: Examines the physical characteristics, behavior, methods
of communication, and ecological significance of ants.
ISBN 0-8234-0771-3
1. Ants—Juvenile literature.   [1. Ants.]   I. Title.
QL568.F7P38   1989
595.79′6—dc19   89-1943   CIP   AC
ISBN 0-8234-0771-3

Contents

4

1

How Ants Look

Hurry hurry, scurry, scurry. Whenever we see ants, they look very active. They march in line across our kitchen floors. They swarm around the openings of their nests. What are all these busy creatures doing?

Army ants on the lookout for food EDWARD S. ROSS

thorax

petiole

abdomen

head

antennae

leg

You can see the head, thorax, and abdomen of this young queen ant clearly, as well as four of the legs, the antennae, and the left eye EDWARD S. ROSS

Ants are insects. Like other insects, their bodies have three parts —a head in front, a thorax in the middle, and an abdomen behind. Ants also have a thin "petiole" joining the abdomen and thorax. All insects, including ants, have six legs. The legs are attached to the thorax.

On its head, an insect has a pair of antennae. The antennae of ants are bent. They are sensitive to touch and odor. If you watch an ant closely, you can see it wave its antennae and touch things with them.

It may seem strange, but ants, like many other insects, have five

small eyes

The three small eyes on top of the head of this bulldog ant are easy to see.
EDWARD S. ROSS

eyes. There is a pair of big compound eyes on the sides of the head. A compound eye is made up of many separate tiny units. Each unit has its own bundle of cells that can sense light. By combining the information from all the units of the eye, the insect's brain can form an image.

The other three insect eyes are small. They can't form images. But they are very sensitive to changes in the intensity of light. The simple eyes, called ocelli (oh-CELL-ee), are located in a triangle on top of the insect's head.

2
Ants Live and Work Together

Ants are closely related to bees and wasps. They vary in size. The tiniest are as small as a dot made by the tip of a pencil. But tropical ants can get very large, sometimes more than an inch long. Like many of their cousins, ants are social insects. They do not live alone. They live together in colonies instead.

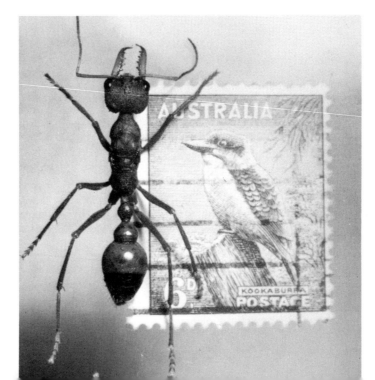

The bulldog ant from Australia is quite large. EDWARD S. ROSS

There are more than 7,600 different kinds, or species, of ants. Some live in small groups with only a few dozen members. Others have enormous colonies of many millions. At a particular time of the year, mature colonies in almost all ant species produce male and female ants with wings. These ants come out of the nest and fly away. The males and females from different colonies mate.

After mating, the female ant loses her wings. She burrows into the ground. Then she prepares a small space for herself that she seals off completely.

In places with cold winters, mating happens in the fall. After making her cozy little chamber, the queen rests there through the winter. In the spring, the queen wakes up and lays some eggs.

The eggs don't hatch into tiny ants. Like many other insects, ants have complete metamorphosis. They go through several stages— egg, larva, and pupa—before they look like ants. The eggs produce little wormlike larvae. This is the queen's first brood.

A queen ant with her first eggs and larvae
EDWARD S. ROSS

The queen takes care of the larvae without leaving her home. Her body breaks down the flight muscles she doesn't need anymore. It also uses stored fat to make food for the larvae. The food is a liquid from the queen's gut. She feeds the larvae from her mouth.

The larvae get bigger and fatter. They molt, or shed their skins, several times as they grow. The last time they molt, they become pupae. The pupae are long and smooth, with rounded ends. They don't feed. Inside each pupa's outer covering, an adult ant is developing.

Carpenter ant nest with larvae and pupae. The pupae are inside cocoons in this kind of ant and some others.
MILAN BUSCHING

pupa

larva

When they are ready, the new ants break out of their pupae. These ants are female, like their mother. But they are sterile. They will never be able to mate. They are called worker ants. Their job is to collect food and take care of the nest, the queen, and her brood.

The ant colony grows slowly at first. Only worker ants are born, and they are all females. As the colony grows, the workers dig new tunnels and new chambers for raising the brood. After a couple of years, the queen lays some eggs that become winged males. These fly away to mate. A few years after that, the colony produces winged females, the future queens of new colonies, as well as males.

Winged leaf-cutter ants ready to leave and mate   MILAN BUSCHING

3

Workers and Soldiers

Once the first workers have taken over the work of the colony, the queen concentrates on laying eggs, and more workers are produced. The youngest workers usually stay inside the nest. They feed the queen and the brood. They lick the bodies of the queen and other workers. They store food and clean the nest.

When they are older, the workers get involved in constructing new nest chambers. Older workers also leave the nest to search for food.

Army ants tend larvae and one pupa in a cocoon that will become males and queens. Notice how much larger these larvae are than the workers.

CARL W. RETTENMEYER, UNIVERSITY OF CONNECTICUT

cocoon

larva

15

Some ants have special kinds of workers. Desert species may have large workers that store liquid food in their abdomens. They are so full they can barely move. When the weather is cool and damp, other workers bring food to these storage ants. When it is hot and dry, the other workers come to them for vital liquid.

There are also ant species that have workers of different sizes. Each size may have its own special job. For example, one leaf-cutter species has large workers that cut and gather leaves. But it has tiny workers, too, that go out with the larger ones. The small ants don't help cut or carry the leaves. Instead, they chase away flies which try to attack the busy larger workers.

A honey ant with liquid stored in its enlarged abdomen
EDWARD S. ROSS

Army ant soldier   EDWARD S. ROSS

Soldiers are ants with large heads and jaws. Only some species have soldiers. There can be different types of these protectors. One kind uses its strong jaws to cut off the legs of enemies. Another type has pointed, hook-shaped jaws that pierce invaders. The third sort uses its large head to block nest entrances.

4

How Ants "Talk"

In a colony, important information must be passed on—"An enemy is invading," or "There's lots of food in that direction." How do ants get across such messages?

The most common way ants "talk" is with chemicals called pheromones. When a worker ant finds good food, it walks home slowly. As it goes, now and then it drags its stinger along the ground. The stinger deposits tiny amounts of a powerful chemical. In this way, the ant lays a scent trail from the food back to the nest.

When other workers discover a fresh odor trail, they follow it away from the nest. Their antennae sweep from side to side as they sense traces of the trail chemical rising from the ground.

When these workers find food at the source, they, too, lay trails back to the nest. The odor along the way becomes stronger and stronger as more workers head back to the nest with food.

Army ants rely on both scent and touch to keep their marching columns together.
© CHIP CLARK

When the food runs out, the workers return without dragging their stingers and adding to the trail. The scent becomes weaker and weaker. Soon, it attracts no more ants. In this way, new workers don't waste their efforts traveling to a food source that has been used up.

When enemies attack the nest, the first ants to meet them release an alarm chemical. Small amounts of the alarm pheromone in some species attract other workers. As the workers get closer to the scene of battle, the amount of the pheromone increases. Then it excites them, sending them into a battle frenzy.

This alarmed acacia ant is raising its abdomen to release a pheromone.
Several different pheromones may be produced in the abdomen.
WILLIAM F. WOOD, HUMBOLDT STATE UNIVERSITY

5

Ants That Farm

Most ants eat many different foods. They search the ground for insects. They lap at the sweet sap of trees. But many ants eat only one kind of food. Some feed just on eggs of other insects. Others prey only on other kinds of ants.

Weaver ants tear apart a bug.
EDWARD S. ROSS

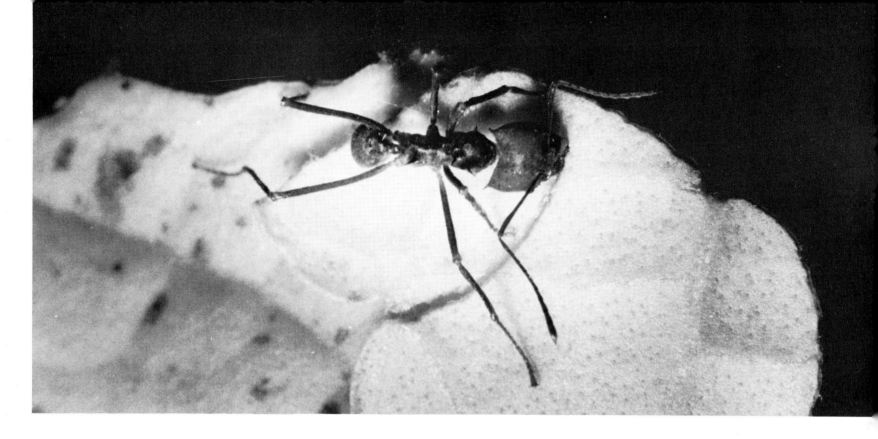

Some of the most successful ants in North and South America don't go out to gather their food. They grow it instead. There are around 200 different kinds of these ants that grow fungus as their only food. Instead of gathering food for themselves, they collect food to feed the fungus that grows inside their nests. Some collect dead insects or pieces of fruit. But most use the leaves, stems, and flowers of plants. They are called leaf-cutter ants.

When leaf cutters go collecting, they can ruin a garden overnight. In many parts of South America, people can't grow vegetable gardens. The ants will harvest them before the people can.

A leaf-cutter ant at work
CARL W. RETTENMEYER,
UNIVERSITY OF CONNECTICUT

23

After large workers bring pieces of plants into the nest, small workers lick the plant pieces and cut them into tiny specks. Then they chew the specks until they are pulpy. The bits of pulp are then placed into the fungus "garden." When new garden areas are begun, workers pluck bits of fungus and "plant" them onto the new garden areas.

The ant funguses are special. They grow fat tips that the ants nip off for food. No other funguses are allowed in the garden. The ants carefully weed out other kinds if they begin to grow.

A leaf-cutter ant nest.
In the center
is a new bit of leaf
with the fungus garden
around it. © CHIP CLARK

*Leaf-cutter ant queen being attended by workers. She is much bigger
than they are.*   CARL W. RETTENMEYER, UNIVERSITY OF CONNECTICUT

When a winged leaf-cutter queen leaves the nest, she tucks a
piece of the fungus into a pouch below her mouth. After she digs her
nest chamber, the queen spits out the fungus. She also lays a few
eggs. She takes good care of the fungus and her brood. She plucks
out bits of the garden and touches them to the tip of her abdomen.
The clear brownish liquid she produces nourishes the fungus like
manure feeds a vegetable garden.

6

Army Ants and Driver Ants

Most ants live in underground nests, but not the tropical American army ants. They stay aboveground on the forest floor or in the lower parts of trees. At night, the tens to hundreds of thousands of army ant workers in a colony link their legs together to form layer upon layer of living chains covering the queen and brood. During the daytime, the workers head out to collect food. Soldiers accompany and protect them.

Instead of living in an underground nest, army ants form a living wall with their bodies to protect the queen and brood. CARL W. RETTENMEYER, UNIVERSITY OF CONNECTICUT

Army ants attacking a longhorned grasshopper EDWARD S. ROSS

The ants attack other animals in their path. They can kill tarantulas, lizards, and nestling birds. They cut their prey apart and carry it back to the bivouac (BIH-vou-ak) site, the place where the queen and brood remain. The brood at this time consists of newly laid eggs as well as pupae that have developed from an earlier batch of eggs.

The colony stays at one bivouac site for about three weeks. The queen's abdomen grows very large very quickly. Then, within a few days, she lays 100,000 to 300,000 eggs! Some workers stay behind to care for the queen and brood while their sisters go out to gather food. After another week or so, the eggs hatch within a few days of each other. The colony is now full of wriggly larvae, and the workers begin to get excited. Now there are no eggs in the colony, only larvae and pupae.

Shortly after the eggs hatch into larvae, tens of thousands of new workers emerge from the colony's pupae. The colony becomes even more bustling. There are more workers to carry out food raids. There are larvae to be fed. The life pattern of the colony changes. The colony is on the move, traveling to a new bivouac site at the end of each day. Well after dark, the queen, whose abdomen is now smaller so she can walk easily, moves to the new home. Several columns of workers and soldiers march with her, protecting her from harm.

When the larvae pupate, the colony once more settles down to one site. The queen grows huge again and lays another gigantic batch of eggs. The cycle has started all over again.

Queen army ant being escorted to a new bivouac site
CARL W. RETTENMEYER, UNIVERSITY OF CONNECTICUT

queen

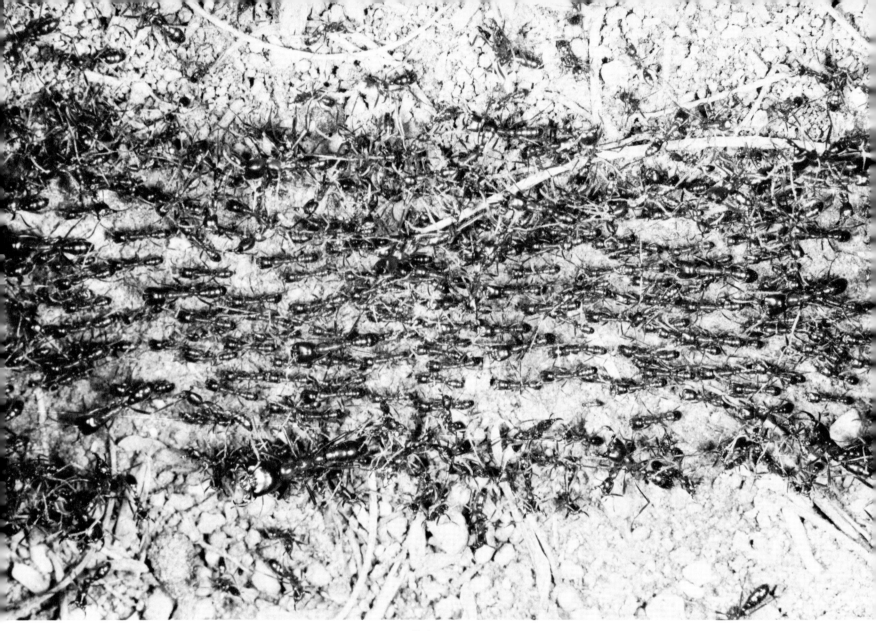

Driver ants   CARL W. RETTENMEYER, UNIVERSITY OF CONNECTICUT

In Africa, driver ants carry out daily raids much like the South American army ants. But driver ant queens always have huge abdomens because they lay eggs at a rate of three to four million each month! These ants dig a nest into the ground where they live for as long as three months. When they move the colony, it takes several days. There may be as many as twenty-two million ants in one colony.

Driver ants successfully attack even larger animals than army ants do. They can kill monkeys or pigs if the animals are trapped. But large animals and people can usually get out of the way of either army ants or driver ants. The stories of them eating everything in their path are definitely exaggerated.

7

Plants That Make Homes for Ants

Ants can be very fierce. They have strong jaws. They can sting. Certain kinds of plants in tropical places have hollow parts that make perfect homes for ants. The ants live in the plants and defend them. Some plants have hollow thorns where ants live. Others have spaces in their stems or trunks that become ant homes.

This plant has spaces inside where ants live. The chamber on the right has been opened to show the ant brood inside.
D. CAVAGNARO/DRK PHOTO

Whistling thorn acacia with hollow lumps where ants live
WILLIAM F. WOOD, HUMBOLDT STATE UNIVERSITY

The whistling thorn acacia of Africa has hollow woody lumps on its branches. Ants bite holes in the bases of the lumps and use them as nests. When a hungry leaf-eater like an antelope nibbles on the leaves, the ants swarm out of their nest and attack. If an insect such as a caterpillar is on the plant, the ants kill it or throw it off.

The acacia not only gives the ants cozy, protected places for raising their brood, it also provides the ants with food. At the base of each leaf, drops of nectar form. The ants visit these spots regularly to eat the nectar.

Some ant plants can't survive without their insect protectors. One scientist removed the ants that live in the hollow thorns of the South American bull-horn acacia. Soon the leaves were chewed up by other insects while nearby plants with ants living in them stayed healthy. The scientist decided that the plants couldn't live for longer than a year without ants to protect them.

Acacia ant feeding on nectar at the base of a leaf
WILLIAM F. WOOD, HUMBOLDT STATE UNIVERSITY

8
Ants and Other Insects

As army ants move through the forest, other creatures go with them. Birds flutter overhead, feeding on the insects flushed out by the raiding columns. Beetles join the colony and feed on the brood. Flies buzz about, scavenging on bits of food left by the ants and sharing food with the ants.

Most insects that travel with army ants just take advantage of the commotion to increase their chances of getting food. But many insects have life cycles closely tied to those of various ant species. Some of these resemble the ants so closely that only a careful scientist will notice the differences. Beetles are especially common as ant companions. Ant-shaped beetles of several species accompany the raiding columns of driver and army ants. They recognize the trail pheromones of their host species. Many such beetles can get the ants to feed them.

Army ant column with workers and soldiers. One arrow points to a beetle that travels with the ants. EDWARD S. ROSS.

Other beetles live in ant nests. They often produce chemicals that fool the ants. One kind wanders near a nest of its host when it is homeless. When it encounters a worker, it offers the tip of its abdomen. The worker feeds on a liquid released from special glands. Then the ant moves to the side of the beetle. There, it feeds on a second chemical. Then it picks up the beetle and carries it into the nest, where it is accepted as a member of the colony.

The insect in the center of this picture is a beetle, not an ant. If you look very closely, you can see some small differences from its ant hosts.
CARL W. RETTENMEYER, UNIVERSITY OF CONNECTICUT

Most of the beetles and other insects that live with the ants do nothing for their hosts. They take food from the ants or feed on their larvae. But ants have insect helpers as well. Aphids and scale insects feed on plant sap. The sap passes through their bodies so fast that they don't remove all the nutrients. They excrete a sweet liquid called "honeydew" from their rear ends. Many kinds of ants take care of aphids or scale insects and feed on the honeydew.

The ants generally care for aphids and scale insects that live on plants near the nest. A few kinds of ants keep them inside the nest where they feed on the roots of plants. To get honeydew, an ant strokes the abdomen of an aphid with its antennae. The aphid responds by secreting a drop of honeydew. If you look closely, you may find ants tending aphids in your own yard. Look for twisted-looking leaves near the tips of branches of trees or other plants. The activities of the aphids often make the leaves curl up.

Ants tending their aphid "cows." EDWARD S. ROSS

9

The Importance of Ants

Ants may be small, but they are among the most important creatures on earth. In most parts of the world, there is actually more total weight of ants than of bigger animals with backbones. Ants are the ruling creatures in the tropics, especially in South America. Early explorers described Brazil as "one great ants' nest."

Even in North America, the number of ants is impressive. In one area of Maryland, scientists counted 73 nests of the most common species covering 10 acres of ground. There were about 12 million workers, and the total weight of the ants was around 210 pounds (100 kilograms). Other ant species, too, lived in the same area.

A fire ant nest in Mississippi. Such a nest can be 3 feet high and house 300,000 ants. U.S. DEPARTMENT OF AGRICULTURE

Ants are very important to the cycles of life. They are among the most important predators on other insects and thus help keep pest populations down. Scientists counted 102,000 insects brought back to a wood ant nest in just one hour. When tree trunks were ringed with grease, keeping ants from climbing into the branches, the trees grew 30 percent less than trees from which ants gathered insects. Ants, in turn, are food for a large number of other animals.

Like earthworms, many kinds of ants help make and turn the soil. Their nests loosen the earth and bring air into it. Some ants collect seeds. The ones they don't eat can sprout and grow into new,

*Ants feed on
a variety of insects.
Here, a worker
drags a cockroach
to the nest.*
CARL W. RETTENMEYER,
UNIVERSITY OF CONNECTICUT

healthy plants. Carpenter ants make their nests in rotten logs. Their activities help speed up the process of decay, returning the wood to the soil more quickly.

But ants can also cause problems. Carpenter ants can damage wood homes. Leaf-cutter ants make farming very difficult in South America. Fire ants from Brazil, which have colonized the American South, are a big problem for farmers. And by tending aphids, ants encourage damage to crop plants.

Ants may be both helpful and harmful to human society. But they are a vital and fascinating part of the natural world.

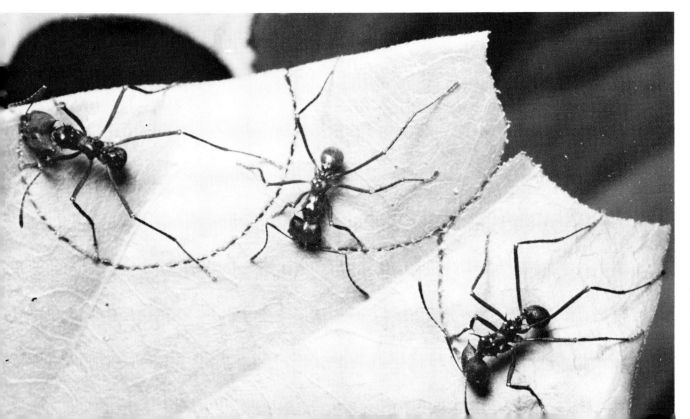

Leaf-cutter ants destroy crops in South America.
EDWARD S. ROSS

Index

(Numbers in *italics* refer to pages with illustrations)